ANTHOLOGY OF POETRY BY YOUNG AMERICANS®

1999 EDITION
VOLUME XCVIII

Published by Anthology of Poetry, Inc.

1999 Edition
Volume XCVIII

Printed in the United States of America

To submit poems
for consideration in the year 2000 edition of the
Anthology of Poetry by Young Americans®,
send to:

Anthology of Poetry, Inc.
PO Box 698
Asheboro, NC 27204-0698

Authors responsible
for originality of poems submitted.

The Anthology of Poetry, Inc.
307 East Salisbury • P.O. Box 698
Asheboro, NC 27204-0698

Paperback ISBN: 1-883931-17-7
Hardback ISBN: 1-883931-21-5

The 1999 edition celebrates our tenth anniversary of publishing the *Anthology of Poetry by Young Americans*®. During our first decade of publishing we have witnessed a resurgence in the popularity of poetry. It is our belief that poetry and children are a perfect fit. They embrace the freedom of poetry and push and pull it in infinite directions exploring every nook and cranny of their life. We have watched some authors published year after year develop and grow. We have watched current events, sports stars, and other celebrities added and dropped from the collective consciousness of our children. We have seen the same themes: concern and delight about nature, thoughts about God, family, pets, and friends, feelings about first loves, and leaving things behind, all explored with the diversity and individuality of each child. Poetry is open to all children at all levels, from the academically gifted to the child-at-risk. Expression is not limited by their developing knowledge of sentence structure, punctuation or form. Poetry can give us a glimpse of each author that is as timeless and specific as any photograph.. We tried to present the poems as the author wrote them, in their format and punctuation.

We would like to extend a special thanks to all the poets who participated. We are expecting great things from them in the future.

The Editors

PLANETS

Planets, are round not making a sound.
Are they up in the air, or on the ground?

Planets, do they have wings? Two have rings.
One has a huge red spot, and another is super hot!

Planets, one has lots of vapors,
and another has plenty of skyscrapers.
One is the smallest size, and one has a surprise,
that it spins on its side!

Planets, the first is closer,
but the third is farther than the first,
and the fourth is probably dying of thirst.

Planets, we have a magnificent solar system
as you can plainly see,
but the rest of the universe remains a mystery.

Alana Bentley
Age: 12

I LIVE IN A WORLD...

I live in a world,
With colors around,
Where blue flowing streams,
Can always be found.

I live in a world,
With people called friends.
The strongest relationships,
Will never bend.

I live in a world,
Where I know I'm loved.
And there's always guidance,
From Someone above.

I live in a world,
Where all are awake.
And on a sunny day,
There's nothing at stake.

I live in a world,
Where technology mocks,
And time is no more,
Than a few broken clocks.

I live in a world,
Where people are kind.
This wonderful world,
Is all in my mind.

I live in a world,
A world of dreams,
In the world I love,
Where nothing is as it seems.

Katie Singleton
Age: 14

I am Lance,
I wear pants
My brother Tanner,
Waves his banner
My dad Freddy,
Is always ready.

Lance Watkins

Pardon me it was
not me it just
it was my food
it just popped
to say hello
and now
it's right
back down
below.

Chase A. Skiles

LOVE BIRDS

Love is like a bird
sitting in a tree
Love is like a river
striving for the sea
Love is like a mountain
far too high to see
Love is like an oak tree
grandest of all trees
Love is like a swan
graceful as can be
Love moves all obstacles
just for you and me

David Alexander
Age: 14

FRIENDS

My friend Kasey
likes to be lacy.
My other friend Kelsey
has a friend named Chelsea.
Wherever they go they are always together.
They will be friends forever.

Molly Kate Fields

WRITING...

My hand flashes across the paper
I have words inside
But I have just one problem,
These words want to hide
My hand is getting tired
It really needs a rest
Read some other poems
'Cause this one's not the best...

Kate Robison
Age: 9

THINGS THAT BUG ME...

When my dad calls me grumpy.
When my potatoes are always lumpy.
When my sister is so bossy.
When my spaghetti is too saucy.
When my grandma give me hugs
When my grandpa give me bugs.
When I get bossed around.
When I fall on the playground.
When they say it's time for bed.
When they say "You look so red."

THAT'S WHAT BUGS ME!!!!

Jessica Joy Huskisson
Age: 8

FIRST FROST

Death is in the air,
The birds aren't chirping now,
The frost came last night.

It comes every year,
This dreaded terrible frost.
I wish it would stop.
It kills bugs and grass also.
Oh, I just wish it would go.

Ty Hoskins

WINTER

Winter is my favorite season.
I love the snow and presents.
Once I got a computer game and a lot of other stuff.
My dad and I went sledding once.
It was really fun.
I have never seen Santa Claus.
Is there really one?
I also like ice skating.
Well I guess I should go now.
Merry Christmas

Caitlin Meryl Putman

MY MIX-MATCH DAY

I woke up in the morning
from my sleeping and snoring.
I felt kind of strange,
I felt kind of weird.
When I looked in the mirror my face was all smeared.
I went downstairs to get something to eat,
that was when I noticed my feet.
They were huge, gigantic over their size.
That's how they were right before my eyes,
I couldn't believe it, "Not true," I said.
I really felt like going back to bed.
My face was smeared, my feet were huge,
I won't believe it, I refuse.
Then suddenly my arms got tiny.
Now I have a reason to get kind of whiny.
My mom woke up, and she exclaimed,
"Oh my gosh, I've lost my brain!"
I told my mother what happened to me,
she said, "Oh golly be!"
I asked her if she could say something positive.
Then I said, "Never mind I'm just going away,
so I don't cause anymore problems today."
I suddenly woke up, it was just a dream,
but just to make sure...
I let out a scream!!! Ahhhhhhhhhhhhhh

Dedicated to: Erin Pollom

Jamie Pollom

SPRING IS HERE

Spring is here and everyone is filled with joy.
Past winter seems like a decoy.
Roses red as firelight blooming all over the prairie.
In the houses children are merry.
Nothing seems wrong in any way.
Good gracious!!! My cat ran away!

Nick McClain

IN THE MORNING

My, my! It's a quarter 'til eight.
Better get up or I'll be late.
Never, ever have I been late.
That's the time I really hate.
Brushing teeth, brushing teeth, is so much fun!
Sooner or later I'll be done.
Making bed, making bed, what a terrible thing to do.
If you don't make your bed
There is no allowance for me and you!
Breakfast, breakfast, what a bunch.
All I can hear is munch, munch, MUNCH!
On the bus the ride is bumpy.
Ouch! My seat is lumpy.
Finally, finally, we're at school.
That's the place that's really cool!

Kelsey Miller

MY SCHOOL

I hear my teacher's voice,
As cheerful as it is
Then I found out there's a quiz
That I didn't study for!

At recess we play,
At bear time we read,
And sometimes we can plant a seed.
We do something different everyday!

S. MacKenna Stone

WHEN I GO TO SCHOOL

When I go to school,
I feel kind of cool,
We have lunch,
Then go to recess and play in a bunch,
Don't forget we have math!
My teacher and I go through it like a path,
I think school is really fun,
And remember, to school
Don't even bring a water gun,
I really like school, but most of all,
I think it is cool!

Samantha Zammit

TREES

Trees
big, beautiful
swaying, laughing, singing
One has knocked over!
decaying, decomposing, dying
brown, dead
Dirt

Neha Yakhmi
Age: 10

THINGS THAT BUG ME...

When my brother tries to boss me around.
When I have to find a word that's compound.
When I lose a soccer game.
When my dad has a bad claim.
When my brother tries to trick me.
When my mom has to show her I.D.
When I feel bad and like a jerk.
When I cannot do all my homework.
When people ask me a thousand times.
When my teacher always makes me rhyme.

THAT'S WHAT BUGS ME!!

Jordan Kleine
Age: 8

Football
rough, tough
catching, throwing, tackling
helmets, balls, hoop, jerseys
shooting, guarding, dribbling
fast, loud
Basketball

Jaskaran S. Heir

NIGHTTIME

The owls hoot and holler,
The mice squeak and run,
For the dark nighttime has begun.

I heard a noise!
Yes, the raccoons are knocking over
Garbage cans in our front lawn!

My eyelids are getting droopy.
I should be asleep.
With all this noise I can't count sheep.

Nighttime is dark.
Nighttime is noisy.
Nighttime is almost over.

Megan Christine Bishop
Age: 9

I CAN'T HELP IT...

I can't help it if I'm green,
I'm very tall and very lean.
My eyes bob in the air,
And become tangled in my hair.
I don't have a single neck,
Who cares, what the heck!
My hands and arms are short,
My brother's name is Bort.
I weigh fifty pounds,
And own twenty hunting hounds.
But I can't help this,
For I'm a Martian!

Leslie Seals

THE BATTLE OF GETTYSBURG
(JULY 1-3, 1863)

As the Confederacy marched into Gettysburg
It started a battle July first through third.
The Union lost the first day,
They retreated right away.
Pickett's charge was on the last day,
Although it failed, it didn't right away.
That was the last drive into Northern soil,
And that really put the Confederacy in a boil.

Connor H. Nolan

THE FIRST THANKSGIVING

I love Thanksgiving.
It is fun.
I wish Thanksgiving was every month.
I hope you love Thanksgiving too.

I wish my friends could come with me.
But they can't because there are too many kids.
There is not enough of food.

But after all they did come.
I was happy and not sad.
Then we were finished.

Tina Holzer
Age: 8

PEOPLE

People, people, people,
Tall people,
Short people,
Skinny, fat, average people,
Small, little, tiny people,
Last of all, best of all,
God's people.

Willie Matis
Age: 11

MY PET RABBIT

I have a pet rabbit and his name is Thumper.
He's a very good jumper.
He's white with brown, gray and black spots.
He has a fluffy tail.
He likes to sniff out trails.

Kaylie Daugherty
Age: 8

THE FIRST THANKSGIVING

The Indians made the turkey.
The pilgrims made the baked beans.
They all ate sardines.
They all had beef jerky.

Henry Hampton
Age: 8

Sometimes I just wonder
If our being's a mistake.
Our peace is just a memory,
Our kindness mostly fake.

Is God proud of His creation?
I wonder even more;
Though He created humans
We created war.

We can be so filled with hate
That we're blind to those in need.
And we cruel people thrive on things
Like killing, scorn, and greed.

Would the world be better
If we humans just weren't there?
We people filled with hatred who've
Forgotten how to care.

I know we have a purpose
And as the future may before us lie,
There has to be a reason.
The one thing I ask is, "Why?"

Melissa M. McMahan
Age: 13

BEE

Oh no! What's that?
Something's caught inside my hat
Oh no! My hat is on my head
I think I would rather be dead
Oh no! It's buzzing in my ear
I do not want to be here
Oh no! It's crawling down my arm
This creature is going to do me harm
Oh no! It is crawling down my thigh
I think I'm going to cry
Oh no! It's on my knee
Why does it have to be me
Oh no! It's on my toe
I really hope it doesn't start to grow
Ouch! It stung me!
I think it was...
A BEE!!!

Megan Brown
Age: 11

S piders have spinnerets
P rey comes into the web
I nsects get caught on the web
D elicious to eat, for the spider, that is
E nemy is a frog
R esting, now ready for another day.

Zachary Alaka
Age: 8

LIFE AS I SEE IT

Winter is coming wearing her frosty, white robe,
Then spring will be next wearing her bright green cloak.
Summer will follow with fun in the sun,
And autumn is last with her leaves all gone.
Yet life continues in this cycle, endless.
Not stopping one day, one moment, to rest.
'Tis why you should be your greatest each day
Or life's way of living will push you out of its way.

And it won't be kind, needless to say,
For us who have been there
We know, we know pain.
But there is a certain forgiveness in life --
To have and to hold
Throughout your endless strife.

That forgiveness is love
To which you must know
It's within yourself, your knowledge, your soul.
For love has the power to save you from life --
To show you light from its darkness,
To keep fighting the fight.

For love is the binding of life as a book,
But don't forget pain, 'tis there if you look.

Kaitlin Beyrau
Age: 13

OUTSIDE

Outside is like everything
it's the wind,
snow,
rain,
moon
and
sun.
It's the green
of the trees.
It's the white
of the flowers.
It's where you
can be free!
The wind is like
God sneezing
and under my
voice I say,
"God bless you.'
The snow is like
God shaving and
I make an angel.
The sun is like
God opening his
eyes wider and wider.
The moon, tells us when
to go to sleep. The rain is
God's tears I say, "Don't cry."
The bugs and animals are
God's creatures not to hurt,
just to look.

Stephanie Bovis
Age: 9

A SPIDER

The spider is on the prey
He was hard at work all day
He has spinnerets to make his web
So he can go out to play.

Isaiah Payton
Age: 8

PEACE IN MIND

The river was rushing cool and crisp like a fog.
Some little insects were bustling
Around a dead rotting log.
People yelling RUN! from a swarming beehive.
At our school's dance everybody does a little jive.
For everything I could not find.
All of this is peace in mind.

Brick Walker

A WONDERFUL TIME

The air so crisp and clean,
the purest place I've ever seen.

The water flows over the rocks,
bubbling softly, wetting my socks.

The liquid sunshine falls from the sky,
dripping off leaves, wetting you and I.

The cabin so big and homey,
I am always far from lonely.

The trees so majestic and tall,
through the woods, I hear their faint call.

The mountains at night, so big and blue,
with wisps of fog floating through.

The Smokies have touched your heart and mine,
we all can reflect on this wonderful time.

Alexandra Cochrane
Age: 10

HARRY THE HORSE

Harry the horse loved to eat wheat stew,
So wheat he grew, and grew, and grew,
And after weeding the field each day,
Harry solemnly slept away,
Then one day he went to weed,
And stopped short,
Not to proceed,
He slapped his thigh,
Oh, me
Oh, my,
For now the wheat touched the sky!

Emily Meadors
Age: 9

ARACHNID

A lways busy spinning a web
R eady to wrap an insect in
A ction
C ircles its prey in silk
H ard at work at
N ighttime
I nvisible strings
D angling, waiting spider.

Meredith Cohen
Age: 8

GOD

When I try to see you
you try to change
the things I do
even though
you are the big man in the sky
I try my best to please you
but if my mom
is not feeling well
I still bless you in
my prayers
even at night in my dreams
I see you when you cross
the sparkling ocean
I see you walking to me
I try my best to please you
I try my best to please you

Ryan Deal
Age: 10

SUGAR

Sugar likes to run
for her it's really fun.
She likes to bark at other dogs
and sit out in the sun.

Jonathan Keeler
Age: 10

My friend died
She was fried
And we all cried
When we found out she died

Tracy Miller

When I fly up to the sky,
I see beautiful stars and the sun.
Then I see all the clouds,
They look so beautiful,
It makes me think of the one.
When I see all the beautiful things,
It makes me want to fly,
I think I should try.

Haley Taylor

MEMORIES

You can hear the rushing river,
And the hornets buzzing.
You can see the grazing deer,
And the children running.

Remembering all the fun,
In your bunk alone.
Feeling sad to leave the place,
What you now call home.

Sarah Kish
Age: 10

S piders are arachnids
P redators that eat smaller bugs
I nsects like flies are their prey
D ay after the day, the spiders work hard
 to weave their webs
E veryday the spiders think about
 how they catch their prey
R eal spiders have spinnerets
 which they use for making web

David Kite

WRESTLING

Wolfpac is back in red and black,
Sting just be everything,
Scott Hall said Wolfpac ain't nothin' at all,
Goldberg is the man,
But I'm a Stone Cold Steve Austin fan,
Hogan is big and bad
But Warrior is awesome and mad,
Scott Steiner is a big whiner,
Rick is gonna really kick,
Undertaker can do an eye thing
And maybe beat Sting,
X-pac has some awesome moves
And Hogan never grooves,
Norton on the floor quote to Raven: Nevermore

Jason Mantel
Age: 10

COOKIES

Do you know what cookies are made of?
They're made of mud, bugs and dirt under rugs...
What what what's that you say?
You don't want your cookies today.
Oh, okay.
Guess what.
I was just pulling your leg.

Jasmine Bartley
Age: 10

ONCE THERE WAS WAR

I stand there,
still as a statue that stares,
A lonely old field deserted around me,
surrounding me with emptiness.
The dull dried leaves once bright
with the freshness of life,
promenade as they plunge to the ground.
Yet this place filled with emptiness
was once alive with war,
an old, forgotten battlefield, not troubled anymore.

I close my eyes and open my mind,
the flame of imagination ignited.
There is a rustle in the trees,
and the Redcoats appear,
so brightly flourished and new.
Their broad bright grins are flashing,
as proud as a well-pruned peacock.
They pull their cannons, shining and fresh,
and hold their rifles by their side.

Advancing through the break in the trees,
come defenders of this land.
Though they are humble soldiers, in ragged raiments
Confidence blesses them too.
They stand apart and hold their muskets,
ready for anything.
Each soldier tries to look sure,
but all have fear hidden in their anxious eyes.

The battle erupts, and the warriors fight on.
I see them tremble one by one and fall,

topple over, struck by hatred.
Blood is everywhere, and people rush to-and-fro.
I hear a frantic scream for help,
And I see the boys, not men, drop to the ground,
The guns never cease, and they keep falling,
falling just like the leaves.
A soul once filled with love and joy, crumpled by death,
fallen never to arise again.

I open my eyes, as to see no more.
A cold and harsh wind begins to blow,
a frigid whisper of harshness,
fighting with my coat and sending shivers up my spine.
The leaves twist on through the breeze,
and I start home again.
The leaves crunch under my feet,
thoughts still run through my mind
Of the poor souls deserted in the battlefield,
left forgotten by the breeze.

Alyssa Scheurle
Age: 13

AUTUMN IS SO PRETTY

Autumn is the season,
It is here right now,
With all the pretty leaves.
Yes, that's the reason,
I love this season.

Brittany Nicole Bezotte
Age: 10

THE VERY BORING DAY

Today is very boring,
my friends are at camp,
we were going to have a cookout,
but today is very damp,
my mom and dad are at work doing lots of stuff,
my brother's home from baseball, doing boring stuff,
my friend Albert came over and asked if I could play,
my brother said no that's okay,
he has to do some homework inside
and cannot go play,
so that's how today went,
I hope this boring day never happens again!

Heather Achterberch
Age: 9

In 1492, Columbus sailed the ocean blue.
He had to beg and wait for years and years.
All the king and queen wanted was money and wealth.
They finally said, "Yes."
They wished him the best,
And Columbus was on his way.
By that time, his hair was gray.
His crew was about to sue.
They were mad the ship smelled bad.
Look, they reached land!
He was glad now, not sad.
He looked around, kissed the ground.
He thought he was in Asia, but little did he know,
He discovered a new land.
And 'til this very day, Columbus is still famous
For discovering our land.

Krista Forgey
Age: 10

CHRISTMAS DAY

Christmas Day
Red and green
Cooked ham
Bells
Cookies
Presents
Christmas Day

Daniel Roper
Age: 7

SPRING

The fresh breeze blowing.
The sound of water flowing.
Fish knowing it's spring.

Andy Lakas
Age: 11

PAM

There once was a girl named Pam.
She liked to eat Spam.
Once she saw a ram
she ran for some Spam.
She gave it to the ram
and was never seen again.

Christopher Wehner
Age: 10

FLOWERS

Flowers need showers
And showers are good
Flowers grow pretty
If I water them good
Don't ask me how they grow,
Don't ask what a seed is,
Just grow one yourself
And you'll see what a seed is
And you'll see how they grow
Does that answer your question
If you had any at all

Amanda Harrison
Age: 9

B all
A wesome
S kill
K ing of basketball
E xcellent
T eriffic
B ounce
A live
L ay-up
L ive through it

Amy Angelini
Age: 9

SUNSHINE

The shine is out
The birds sing a beautiful song
The flowers blossom bright
Then the sunshine fades into night

Kelsey Springman
Age: 9

THE SEASON OF FALL

Fall is such a ball,
And I can give my friends a call.
We can jump in the leaves,
In the cool fall breeze,
That is why fall is such a ball!

Margaret Stalbaum

EGGS

First you buy eggs
Then you take the eggs home
Then cook the eggs
Then you'll have to set the table
Then you eat the eggs.

Seth Councell
Age: 8

MY SUBJECTS

Basketball
Is fun and soccer
Is too, but my
Favorite subject
Is looking at you

Anthony Stahl

GRAVITY

Gravity.
It's a force.
It summons me towards the ground.
It seems as though the ground is rushing at me.
I am falling towards the earth.
It's like zooming in on a small picture of reality.
It gets bigger and bigger.
A cloud.
Another one.
White haze.
It's clear again.
The ground approaches quickly.
It looks as though I will splat on the pavement.
Gravity grabs at me even more
And pulls me towards the ground.
I am about to confront the earth face to face.
POOF!
My parachute springs out towards the sky above me.
It tears at the wind and clutches it.
I am slowly lowered to the ground.
THUD!
I am on the ground.
I look up.
The parachute is slowly lowering towards me,
Also under gravity's power.
It soon envelops me like a blanket.
It is all around me.
I would like to be skydiving again.

Daniel O'Day
Age: 14

THE FOUR SEASONS

I love all four seasons.
They give me many reasons
To enjoy myself all year long.
When spring comes, it means the end of school.
That means I can spend my summer at the pool.
Falltime is fun to play in the leaves,
That come tumbling down from the trees.
When winter comes it brings a cold freeze,
Snow and holidays are
My most favorite time of the year.
That is why the changing seasons are so dear.

Jaclyn Zurbriggen
Age: 8

THE JOG

A frog and a hog were on a jog
Then they came to a log
The frog jumped over the log
The hog couldn't
He pushed, and pulled
But it wouldn't move
Then he dug under the log
And he was on the other side
Then they continued their jog

Sara Tokoly
Age: 8

WINNIE THE POOH

Pooh is cute, weird, and funny.
Sometimes he eats too much honey.
He has a lot of friends.
His friendships never end.

Amber Hart
Age: 9

MY SISTER LILY

I have a sister named Lil
At home we call her a pill
Our baby Lily
Is sometimes so silly
And love her we always will.

Ellen Kapitan

THIRD GRADE

T hird grade is hard
H ey! No running down the hall!
I love third grade
R eady or not. Here I come
D oing our best is what we do.

G ee I missed the part
R eady to get started on English
A boy got hurt
D o you do your best
E verybody loves third grade.

Scott Rutherford
Age: 9

BUDDY

Buddy is my puppy.
He's not always lovey.
We like to play dress-up.
But we always mess up.
We run around the house.
Buddy's scared of a mouse.
We dig outside.
We come back with pride.

Alexis du Bernard
Age: 8

GIRLS

Girls think they are so cool
But they can be really cruel
I wish they would be nicer to me
Because if they don't I'll make them pay a fee

Rachel Smith
Age: 9

MY FAMILY

My family loves me.
I care for my family.
I love my family.
We love each other.
We care for each other.

Renee Kaplan

Mom
nice, fun
loving, caring, funny
She cares and cooks for me.
Loving person

Ben Genova
Age: 11

GOATS

I have goats.
They are fun and nice animals.
But sometimes they are wild,
like my sister's goat, Maria.
She is wild and she is funny,
and sometimes she's just silly.
My goat's name is Bambi.
She is strong and tough and rough.
But usually she is pretty nice.
Maria usually is the one who pulls people.
Bambi usually is the calm one.
Really, they are just like kids.

Eric Kutemeier
Age: 9

MY DOG BITSY

She likes to play ball everyday
and she likes to swim away.
She plays with her friend Wisky
and eats bones everyday.
She's black and fuzzy and very fancy.
She has brown eyes like the brown dark dirt.
But after a long day she sits and lies
and she falls asleep by my side.

Nancy Lesniewski
Age: 10

TEACHERS

Teachers are great.
What's eight times eight?
They'll always be your mate.
Because teachers are great.
And the answer's forty-eight.

Amanda Schaaf

Me
smart, brilliant
shining, loving, helping
smart, intelligent, quick, young
boring, snoring, wrinkling
old, sick
Dead

Adam Momcilovic
Age: 10

MY BABY COUSIN

Cute
funny, lovable
charming, beautiful, pretty
sweet, caring, adorable, nice
Ashley (Goog)

Brittany Smoter

BABY

Baby
small, nice
running, laughing, playing
He won't stay put.
Toddler

Brandon Joseph Gomez
Age: 11

MOTHERS

Mothers are great.
Mothers help you
When you are sick.
They help us tie your shoes
When we are little.

Peter Bergstrom

Summer
hot and humid
kids swimming, sun shining
sun keeps you warm in this season
Sunny

Sean Kelly
Age: 10

Crayons
brand new
coloring, marking, drawing
school, C.C.D., home, grandma's
breaking, wearing, cracking
old, broke
Trash

Leanne Marcheschi

BLAKE

B oy, he plays hard!
L ikes to play soccer
A thletic boy
K ick the ball hard!
E xcellent goal!

Blake Baugh
Age: 10

HORSES

Horses are beautiful,
Horses are nice,
Horses are better,
Horses are cool,
You can say that I like horses a lot.

Amanda R. Fusner

NOISES IN THE NIGHT

I sit alone by the candlelight
With book in hand on a windy night.
Inside, all is cool and calm
But outside the wind keeps blowing on.

From somewhere inside I hear a creak,
A trod, a tiptoe, the sound of feet.
I think to myself, am I not alone?
My heart starts to beat for my fear has grown.

Could this someone be my foe?
The answer to this question I have to know.
So from my seat I slowly rise.
The candle flickers and suddenly dies.

In the dark I now feel nothing but fear
As I hear the creaking drawing near.
I run and grope to find the light
For I desperately need to regain my sight.

I flick on the light and what do I see?
Nothing but my book and me.

Carrie Drapac
Age: 15

MY HERO

I have known my hero all my life.
I never really realized he was my hero.
My hero has saved my life in many ways.
He has saved me from my horrible past.
My hero has saved me from starting
to hate someone I didn't want to hate.
My hero helps me understand things
that I never understood, or thought about before.
I really love my hero.
My hero has helped me
through the hardest times in my life.
I will always love my hero.
My hero is my loving dad.
I love you Dad.

Raquel Siañez
Age: 13

THE SUN

The sun is bright and shiny,
Up close it looks all spiny.
I run around under it all day,
I throw a ball and I play.
Once in a while I get burned,
Since it happened, I have learned.

Andrew Halliar

DOLPHINS

All dolphins red and pink
Come together to link
Across the ocean and across the bay
They come to keep the hurricanes away

Nicky Strazzabosco
Age: 11

MY MOM

My mom is the one who loves me all day.
What she is feeling I can always say.
She is the one who helps me too
On homework, games, and even tying my shoes.
My mom's rules I will always obey.
I love you, Mom.
I'll love you always.

Phillip G. Morales

MY MOM IS THE BEST

Mom is the best.
She never rests.
She puts me to bed.
She knows that my favorite color is red.
Sometimes she misses me.
Sometimes she kisses me.
She likes to read to me.
She likes to feed me.
And that is my mom.
She's like a bomb.
That explodes with love.
Like a dove.

Jamie Doolittle
Age: 9

GUSSY

Gussy's my name.
Softball's my game.
I throw really fast and run like the wind.
My uniform's black and blue
Like my body after the game.
But my friends tell me Gussy,
You're okay, even for a
Freckled-face girl.

Ashley Bowling
Age: 10

WHY, OH WHY?

I wish I were a bluebird, up in the sky.
Every day would be a natural high!

Children would look gaily at me.
A cute little bird is the life to be.

The view up there would really be great.
The big blue sky every morning would await.

I can see me now,
Perched on a bough.

Sitting so straight,
With nothing to hate.

But I am not a bluebird up in the sky.
I am just a young girl wondering why...
Some are born to walk and others to fly!

Patricia Whitener

CRAYONS

I don't like to draw at all,
Ever since I got caught drawing on the wall.
Now I hate to draw with crayons.

Ryan Lorance
Age: 9

THE BACKSTABBER

The witch behind the pretty face,
With beady eyes and frilly lace,
Can suck you in with generosity,
And then turn on you with animosity.
She chooses her prey very wise,
And then alienates you by telling you lies.
Once you're in it's hard to get out,
And she will do it again without any doubt,
So stay clear of people
Who are too friendly and too kind,
Because they might just play games with your mind.

Colleen Musielak

HUNTING

Today I saw a deer,
Living in the woods always in fear,
To the sound of a gun,
Always alert and ready to run,
When the hunter gets the deer in his sight,
The deer better run because of his fright,
'Cause when he feels the sting of the hunter's lead,
He knows he is dead.

Nicholas Yukon

FRIENDS

Friends are cool.
They go with you to school.

Friends are neat,
a lot of times they are sweet.

Friends are nice.
They don't like mice.

Friends stand up for you
when you're feeling blue.

Friends are loud.
We are all proud.

Friends really care.
They always want to share.

Fiends are like a keepsake
from night to daybreak.

Friends are fair.
They are like a teddy bear.

Friends are keen,
but sometimes mean.

Friends like what you like
especially riding a bike.

Jessica McFarlane

SHOOTING STARS

Shooting stars going across the sky
So quickly, so silently.
Make a wish and wish it well.
Wish of love or wish of money?
Either one to me.
Make sure your heart's desire is your wish.
The wrong one may be fatal.
Shooting stars going across the sky
So quickly, so silently.
Oh shooting star of mine.

Kristin Matushek

MY PUPPY

My puppy's name is Nellie
I love her very much
She has a chubby belly
And she's cuddly to the touch.

She plays with me and runs all day
Sometimes she jumps with glee
I will never give her away
She means the world to me!

Nicole Brown
Age: 9

LAUREN

Loving, kind, friendly
Who wishes to be a dancer.
Who dreams of doing good in everything.
Who wants to feed the hungry.
Who wonders why people can't get along.
Who fears death.
Who is afraid of fire.
Who likes being loved.
Who believes in friendship.
Who loves pizza.
Who loves to dance.
Who loves softball.
Who loves ice cream.
Who plans to get good grades.
Who plans to give to the poor.
Who plans to be a teacher.
Who will love forever.

Lauren Charbonneau
Age: 10

WINTER SNOW

The streets are icy
The snow is cold on the ground
Trees are very bare.

Aimee Fredericks
Age: 11

Nice
Kind
True

Wishes to meet a space alien.
Dreams of making progress.
Wants to have a dog.
Wonders if there is life on Mars.
Who fears rats.
Who is afraid of mice.
Who likes people that are nice.
Who believes in God.
Who loves candy and bread.
Who loves to play basketball.
Who loves spelling and math.

Brittany Lynn Smith
Age: 10

MY NEW BROTHER STEVE

One fine Christmas Eve,
I got a new brother named Steve.
His birthday is in December,
His birthday I'll always remember.
Even though he picks his nose,
He wears cool clothes.
I love my brother,
I don't do diapers so there's always my mother.

Jennifer De Young
Age: 10

ANGIE KRISTOFF

Friendly
Nice
Sweet
Wishes to fly to South Carolina.
Dreams of dogs.
Wants to go to college.
Who wonders what space is like.
Who fears bad dreams.
Who is afraid of monsters.
Who likes dogs.
Who believes in Jesus.
Who loves dogs.
Who loves chicken poppercosh.
Who loves fortune cookies.
Who plans to go to college.
Who wants to live to be one hundred.

Angie Kristoff
Age: 10

DOLPHINS

All dolphins red and pink
Come together to link
Across the ocean and across the bay
They come to keep the hurricanes away

Nicky Strazzabosco
Age: 11

MY BASEBALL HAT

My favorite hat is very special.
Now I'll tell you why.
It was my very first hat.
That hat is very old, you see.
It is crumpled and dirty, and out of shape.
I still like it.
But now it doesn't fit anymore.

Nick Stepnoski
Age: 10

CLOUDS

C louds are cool!
L ook at the bunny-shaped one!
O ooo there's an airplane!
U p and down, they're everywhere!
D o the clouds move?
S ome are shaped like things!

Samantha Reilly

WHO ARE WE?

Are we people who were created
By some super human being,
Or are we people who were created
By a big bang and dust?

Are we monkeys that evolved into humans,
Or are we living cells that evolved into humans?

Are we life on the brink of destruction,
Or are we a dream?

Will we wake up, and
Life will cease to exist?

Mike Michelin
Age: 12

SPRING

Spring brings April showers.
Washing down those ant hill towers.

Flower patches are everywhere.
Don't ruin them if you dare.

The sun shines on the flowers.
Giving them extra powers.

Ashley Lynn Barath
Age: 11

FOOTBALL

A rough sport
With tackles as hard as rock and
Blocks as rough as sandpaper.

You need skill to survive,
Strength to manhandle your opponents,
Speed for smokin' the challengers.

Football is my favorite sport.
Not everyone can play it,
And only the strong survive.

Richard J. 'Ricky' Hanft
Age: 12

SNOW

The sky gets dark as the deepest cave.
It starts to fall slowly, faster, faster.
It's as free as a bird and light as a feather.
The purest of whites
And every shape different.
The ground starts to freeze, and flowers die out
All because of this little thing,
This tiny feature,
That we know as snow.

Ellie A. Hansolte
Age: 12

FLOWERS

Flowers come out on the loveliest spring day;
They always look so bright and gay.

Flowers smell so sweet and divine;
I wish, I wish they could be all mine.

Flowers can be scattered or in rows;
They don't have to be in a certain pose.

Flowers are beautiful wherever they are;
Each one is its own beautiful star.

I love flowers of every kind;
They are all special in my mind.

Mindy Kuiper
Age: 13

Money
Power
Greed
Equals
Stupidity
Destruction
Death

Adam Kosior
Age: 13

QUESTIONS

Why does the world live in hatred?
Why can't people get along?
Why are so many people prejudiced?
Why do people judge people by their race?
Why do people murder other human beings?
Why do people do drugs?
Why do people take their own lives?
Why do people feel alone when there are
Millions of people around them?

These questions are asked everyday,
But nobody has a real answer for them.

Brianna O'Keefe
Age: 13

FEAR

What is fear?
Where does it go?
Does it bounce around from person to person
like a grasshopper?
Does it scatter around
like a butterfly?
Or is fear
like a hawk looking for prey to hunt down?
What is your fear?

Anne Kvarta
Age: 13

WHY?

There I sat, before me she lay.
I wondered what would happen to her today.

  Death was growing nearer;
  Her life was getting short.

As she lay there, motionless, I thought,
No matter what, I have to keep fighting.
But I couldn't,
I could not stop crying.

  So there I sat next to her bed,
  I took her hand and said,
      "You cannot leave me now,
      Not when I have not grown up.
      Who will show me right from wrong?
      Or how to write a lovely song?"

Even though you might leave me now
I will soon be with you again.
So good-bye for now,
I will miss you dearly.

Stephanie M. Zimny
Age: 13

THE MESSY SCHOOL

On the first day of school:
It was a mess inside -- I tell you!
Books on the floor, papers here and there.
Chairs down.
Clocks not working -- nothing is!
The lunch is cold, milk is warm.
All the classes are a pig pen.
All the teachers messed up the computers.
Chalkboard messed up -- one here and another there.
Everything is everywhere!

Oh, you should see the office.
It was messier than the whole school!

Martha Bush
Age: 8

WARNING:

America's greatest nighmare
Killing, Manslaughter, Terrorism: problems of America.
Men, Women, Children: Victims of Violence.
When will all the rage end?

The bottom line...
Save a life!

Jayme Saulters
Age: 13

SCHOOL, OH SCHOOL

School, oh school
How much I love you.
You're the greatest place that ever existed!
I love everything in you.

School, oh school
I love all teachers and stuff like that.
I love to do homework and stuff like that.

School, oh school
I don't know what I could do with you!
Oh no! Don't you say it's Saturday.
Oh man, no school --
But Monday I can drive everyone crazy!

Yes! Yes! Yes!

Morgan O'Donnell
Age: 8

BUTTERFLY

Fluttering so freely in the first light of morn,
Beautiful colors so elegantly adorn.
The exquisite movement you make intrigues me,
Full of ecstasy you fly so freely.
As illuminating as the sunrise;
You're as delicate as lace,
You're the symbol for love and a token of grace.

Ashley Ritz
Age: 13

MY STUFFED ANIMAL

I had a stuffed animal
He sat on my shelf
If you want to know what he is
He is an elf.
One day he started to walk
Then he started to talk!!!
First he said my name is Do
Your name must be Who.
My elf is really funny
But I wish he was a bunny.
I really like my elf
I hope you do too
There is one thing I know
My name isn't Who!!!

Katie Elish
Age: 8

I WISH I HAD A FISH

I wish I had a fish
That weighs like a dish and has a wish.
Then he can say it is a beautiful day.
He sings like a wing.
Then he dances to the moon like a toon.

Kevin M. Franchetti
Age: 8

Football
Chicago Bears
helmet kneepads jersey
kick receive tackle guard
Touchdown

Javier Bojorquez
Age: 10

THE BAD STUFF ABOUT READING

Reading stinks
It is boring
It is hard
If two people could do it --
It would be great
Then I could sleep
It would feel good
Well I got to go read
I mean, listen
Wait a second!
There's still more!
It is bad because it is so hard
I wish I could flush it down the toilet --
Then no more books

Tim Gyure
Age: 8

WISH

Did you ever wish you could be a hero?
Saving the village from a dragon,
Saving people from the fire,
Saving the planet from destruction like Superman,
Or just finding the bank robbers?

Did you ever wish you could be a movie star?
Fighting villains one after one,
Making people laugh with joke after joke,
Impressing everyone
With stunt after stunt like Jackie Chan,
Or maybe just being the co-star?

In that case, good luck in becoming a heroic,
Dragon-fighting, fire fighting, planet-saving,
Famous, tough and comical stuntman.
Or just be yourself
Because I know you can.

Mark Rushakoff
Age: 13

HOCKEY

The ice is thick,
You have a graphite stick.
The puck is hit with a flick,
But your goalie is quick.
There's been awarded a penalty shot for number five.
He goes left right until you make the goalie take a dive.
The shot takes flight,
It goes in.
We're destined to win.
There's a minute eight.
The other team is going in straight.
What a shot,
It's blazing hot.
Your goalie goes to a pose called butterfly.
The shot is high.
You lift your goalie glove,
The puck soars in like a dove.
The game is done.
Another win for the robbers of the sun.
The championship is won with no bologna.
Out will come the zamboni.

Ryan Nowak
Age: 12

I'M HUNGRY

What's to eat,
What's to eat?
Maybe if I check the freezer,
I could find some meat
What's to eat,
What's to eat?
If only I could find something,
That would be neat
What's to devour,
What's to devour?
Why can't I eat something,
At this hour?
When's dinner,
When's lunch?
If only I had bananas,
I could eat a whole bunch
What's for breakfast,
What's for brunch?
I'm leaving,
I'm going to munch
I'm out of here,
I'm going around to roam,
I can't believe I just wrote this poem!

Stephen Zacny
Age: 12

WONDERFUL WORLD

As I watch the snow,
Fall to the ground,
and listen for the bells,
what a wonderful sound!!
I sit there and smile,
and think for a while,
what a wonderful place to be!

The children play,
all night and all day,
passing the time away.
They play in the snow,
they don't want it to go,
but that's how it is anyway.
As I sit there and smile,
and think for a while,
what a wonderful place to be!!

The snow is gone,
but there's nothing wrong,
the flowers come today!
I sit there and smile,
and think for a while,
what a wonderful place to be!!

It is now spring,
when people laugh and sing,
awaiting the day,
that they can say,
summer has come our way!
I sit there and smile,

and think for a while,
what a wonderful place to be!!

Summer has come,
the cold is done,
we're going swimming today!
It's about a hundred degrees,
everywhere there are bees,
but nobody pays any mind.
For that they know,
that soon in time,
it's going to be snowing again!
I'm swimming with a smile,
but thinking all the while,
what a wonderful place to be!!

Fall is near,
but don't you fear,
it isn't too cold yet!
The leaves have now,
fallen to the ground,
making a rustling sound.
The children play,
throughout the day,
in every possible way.
I watch with a smile,
and think for a while,
what a wonderful place to be!!

What do you know,
it's starting to snow!
Please, please, snow some more!
I want to play,
in the snow all day,

and build snowmen,
times two or three.
It's been a whole year,
I'm glad to be here,
in this wonderful place we have!!!

Gina Rayson
Age: 12

MY ROOM

As I lie on my floor looking at my ceiling,
I look at the new coat of paint
Over the old one that was peeling

I look at the mirror and I can see a reflection,
It is my lava lamp but only a section

I watch as the lava and liquids intermix,
And just below there are little orange flicks

That is my candle shining so bright,
I look over and see another sight

There is my incense burning and my shell collection,
I stand up and give my room a full inspection

With my walls purple and my ceiling white,
My room suits me just right

Robyn Wolak
Age: 12

EVERYDAY

Everyday I see two kids
wake up to eat the breakfast their mom made.
Everyday I see those kids just make the bus,
but with no shoes on,
or with their hairbrush in their hand.
Everyday I see Mom leave to work
worrying if she'll make it there on time.
Everyday I see the mailman pass by the window
carrying a big sack of mail and smiling.
Everyday I see Mom come home from work
finding her kids quietly and happily watching TV.
Everyday I see Mom make a delicious dinner
while the kids set the table together.
Everyday I see Dad come home from work
and the kids running happily into his open arms.
Everyday I see that family
sit down to eat dinner and talk about their day.
Everyday I see Mom and Dad
walk into each of the kids' rooms
to kiss them good night.
I am just a rusty chandelier
hanging from the dining room ceiling,
but I see a lot from where I hang.

Jennifer Rebecca Morales
Age: 12

A SNOWFLAKE'S WONDER

When a snowflake hits your nose
You can tell the snowflake's froze
From the raindrop it used to be
The finished product now you see.

Down, down, down comes the flake
White and beauty in its wake.
You see its family on the ground
Heard by not a single sound.

You gaze in awe as you stare
at the snowflakes, snowflakes everywhere.
You calmly say, quietly under your breath
"To miss their beauty is worse than death."

Brian McCord
Age: 12

Spring
flowers butterflies
sun birds bees
bugs trees green fun
Visits

Penny Nicole Baldridge
Age: 9

LEAVES

In the autumn the leaves fall
But do not bawl
Because they'll be back
In a great big sack.

Leaves are great
Leaves are grand
They don't play in a band
But if you pile them up
And throw them in the sky
You'll have fun by and by.

Matthew Jones
Age: 10

MR. SNOW

Wet, damp, icy, cold
These things describe the snow
It comes in flakes
Lands on your face
And now your face is cold
You build a snowman
He talks to you
About the things you do
He says he's melting
You put him in the freezer
Then you shut the door
Now he won't melt
Forever, or more

Andrew Jones
Age: 11

OPENING NIGHT

The sound of people talking
The sound of footsteps walking.
Then it all quiets down,
Until there is no sound.
The music starts to play.
The curtain starts to sway.
It opens with a breeze,
And I walk on stage with ease.
I say my first line,
And then I feel fine.
I made it through the whole play,
And at the end all I could say
Was, “At first it was a fright,
But now I can't wait for tomorrow night!”

Lauren Ashley Brechner
Age: 11

MY ROOM

I really hate my room
for Christmas I think I need a broom.
I need a broom for that ugly mess
which includes clothes on the floor from when I dress.
My room is full of dust
I don't want to clean it but my parents say I must.
The mess is so big there is no room to walk
there's not even room to talk.
I have lost the battle lost the war
because now I have to pick up the floor.
I must keep fighting yes I must
but that was wrong I now have to dust.
So if you have to clean your room
PLEASE CLEAN IT VERY SOON!

Jimmy Dempsey
Age: 11

LIVE TO PLAY

To kick the ball with all your might
Send it soaring to an amazing height
See the pigskin fly through the upright
I live to play FOOTBALL!

To hit the ball with all your might
Send it soaring to an amazing height
A grand slam homer would be all right
I live to play BASEBALL!

To shoot the ball with all your might
Send it soaring to an amazing height
A half court shot makes quite a sight
I live to play BASKETBALL!

Whether it's spring, winter or fall
You will find me playing ball
Can't make a choice, I love them all
I live to play SPORTS!

Colton Stombaugh
Age: 10

THE WONDERFUL WORLD

As I look out my window,
I see the great big world in front of me.
The world is a great big beautiful ball,
To me.
I want this world to last,
I want this world to stay,
I want this world forever.
Can someone help me?
I need your help
And together we could make this world better,
And people would see,
That we need this world
Oh please help me.
I'm crying out to you,
And you and you,
I'm crying out to everyone,
I need you.
Oh please help me,
You surely see,
That we as a group,
And me,
Could make this world better,
For us.
We as a group,
Can work together,
We can make it all better.
Oh please would someone help me?
Oh dear,
Oh my,
I think I might cry.
There is no one that will help me,
So I guess it's over,

I'm sorry dear earth,
I can't do it all,
But you are a wonderful great big ball.
Wait one minute,
One more try,
Won't someone help me?
I'm begging,
Please help me.
Can't you see?
Please oh please,
Someone anyone?
Would you please?
Don't you care,
About the air?
The earth,
The dirt,
Don't you care,
About yourself?
I know I do.
I'm asking,
I am begging,
I am pleading,
I need you.
Well thanks anyway.

Amy Mahler
Age: 10

Summer
hot fun
playing swimming hiking
July June December February
sledding skiing ice skating
cold fun
Winter

Jonathan Biancardi

RUGRATS

If you want to mess with the Rugrats,
You have to rap
Because it's Rugrats that
Sit it
Hit it
Fill it

Kyle O'Connor

THE FAT TURKEY

There was a fat turkey
Who got even fatter
Some people thought
He was the Mad Hatter

They tried to kill him
But he climbed up a ladder
They got madder and madder
The turkey got badder and badder
And the people got sadder and sadder.

Timothy Stanis
Age: 9

ZOOMERICKS

Lions, tigers, and monkeys too,
and a bear with a low IQ.
In the middle of the winter,
the elephant got a splinter,
and the lions, tigers, and monkeys got the flu.

Once there was a monkey named Bongo.
Who loved to do the congo.
He got into bed,
and bumped his head.
Now he's really doing the mombo.

There once was a boy named Freddy,
he had a bear named Zeddy.
He went too close to the tigers' den
and dropped the bear in their pen.
Now he has a shredded teddy.

Jonathan D. Dirst
Age: 12

Friendly
Loving
Funny
Wishes to be a pro football player
Dreams of being like Mark McGwire
Wants to own a Camaro
Who wonders of Hawaii
Who fears failure
Who is afraid of not having a job
Who likes Goldberg
Who believes in Jesus
Who loves playing football
Who loves wrestling
Who loves cheese
Who loves his family
Who plans to go to college
Who plans to have a nice car
Who plans to have a nice house
Whose final destination is the Football Hall of Fame

Derek Marich
Age: 11

GRANDMA'S HOUSE

I see Grandpa, Grandma and George
I hear footsteps, cooking and friends
I smell food and Grandma's perfume
I touch the remote and homework pencils
I feel relaxed, good and healthy

Adrian Pulido

THE WAY THE WIND BLOWS

I see a field of wildflowers.
I hear birds chirping and the wind whistling.
I smell wildflowers and fresh grass.
I touch two kittens and a puppy.
I feel like I could fall asleep.

Emily Fields

AT THE CITY OF CALIFORNIA

I see cars,
I hear people,
I smell trees,
I touch money,
I feel great.

Tim Cogdill
Age: 9

HEAVEN

Heaven is the place where people go,
Their bodies go, head to toe.
Your angel is waiting for you.
One more thing,
Heaven is never old, always new.

Jennifer Tuel

I LOVE GERBILS

I love gerbils don't you know.
They are very cute.
They sleep in the day and play in the night.
They're nocturnal I hoped you knew.
So don't pull on their tail, you'll break it!

Daniel Cebulski
Age: 8

THANKSGIVING IS...

Thanksgiving is a time for tradition
a very good holiday
it is a very big feast
a wonderful day
it is a very thankful day

Bryan Robison

Basketball
Free throws
Jump shots score
Make it go in
Run

Bruce Alexander Jr.
Age: 10

WORLD PEACE

I see children playing happily,
a bright blue sky,
fresh flowers blooming in open fields,
and non-polluted air.
I hear birds chirping, and children laughing.
I smell cookies fresh from the oven.
I touch a baseball bat.
I feel great.

Keegan Kiral

THAT'S WHAT HAPPENS WHEN I BRUSH MY TEETH!

At 9:55 I walk down the hall
and turn into the bathroom.
I pick up my toothbrush
and open the cabinet with a squeak.
I put the toothpaste on the toothbrush.
I pulled it to my mouth and started to brush.
It goes swish, swish through my mouth.
I turn on the faucet,
as the water comes out with a shhhhhhhh!
I tap my toothbrush on the side of the sink.
It goes tick, tick, trick.
Then I set my brush in the holder.
With a bing, bing, and I'm done!

Jennifer R. Anderson
Age: 10

IF I WERE A SPICE GIRL

If I were a Spice Girl I'd sing all day.
If I were a Spice Girl I'd swim by the bay.

If I were a Spice Girl, I'd have a show.
If I were a Spice Girl, I'd wear a bow.

If I were a Spice Girl, I'd be Ginger Spice
If I were a Spice Girl, I'd love to play dice.

I think Spice Girls are cool.
If I were a Spice Girl, I wouldn't go to school.

Nicole Kuech
Age: 9

FISHING AT THE COTTAGE

Every time I go to the cottage
I take my dog and I go fishing.
When my dog bites my pole,
I stop her and tell her no.
I cast it back out
and wait until I get a bite.
When I get a bite,
I pull the rod up and wheel it in.
I give it to my dog.

David Sivak
Age: 9

FUN

F un is playing in the sun,
U nder the trees and falling leaves!
N ight comes with a stormy fright,
so we must say, "Good night".

Steven Herrera

JANET JACKSON

Janet Jackson is so kind.
She is a favorite singer of mine.
Her songs make me want to sing.
Because they have a certain ring.

Kylie Sanders
Age: 9

THE FUTURE OF US CHILDREN

The future of us children
Belongs with all the rest
Of the parents in this world
Who are trying to do their best.

Our parents feed and shelter us,
And do this in every way,
So we as children can be fine adults,
That our parents are proud of someday.

For the future of us children
God's love for us is always there,
To live in this great big world,
For all of us to share.

Emily M. Markovich
Age: 8

Books are cool! I'll read chapter books,
I'll read about schnooks,
and I'll read about cooks, and "mook".
If I stay awake
I might read about Jake (the hollow rake).
Sometimes I can read in my room,
but I can never read in an earthquake.
Why not you say?
Because my book would smash in a flash,
and I'd say "hey!"
That was my book to read today,
but I'll get you a book.
He'll say "yes" in a deep voice
and I'll say: good choice, and I'll get him a book.
He and I , I and he shall read, read, read, read and read.
I am going to take it that he likes reading too,
that reminds me I'll read about a dirty old shoe too.
He says it's time to go home, but me n-a-a!
I'm staying right here in this big, big dome,
but he took me home.
So I read in my bed as the moon came out.
As I read my mind is thinking about
what I'll read when I'm a scout.

Dustin Randal Heath

THE MONTHS OF THE YEAR

In January it's so nice because you
drink hot chocolate almost every single night.

In February you have my birthday in the snow,
then we have a snowball fight all night.

In March almost all the snow is gone,
when it gets really dark outside I get a fright.

In April it's so very nice because all the snow is gone,
and there won't be anymore snowball fights.

In May it's so graceful because you get
to eat a normal meal instead
of just chicken noodle soup.

In June it's only one more month until,
it's the Fourth of July so we can
scoop candy and soup.

In July Whew! man is it hot out here!
but is sure is so much fun, but man am I pooped.

In August it's my sister's birthday party,
and everyone came over to go in the pool.

In September it's my cousin's birthday,
at the end of the day it's very cool.

In October we wait for Halloween
and maybe I'll be a ghoul.

In November we skate on the ice.

In December it feels kinda nice.

Barbie A. Foster
Age: 9

SEASONS

Spring is my favorite season
For this I have many reasons,
I love to watch the flowering plants,
While they do their springtime dance.
Summer is a very warm feeling,
Sometimes my skin burns and I begin peeling.
In fall, the trees begin to lose their leaves,
I hope I don't get stung from the bees.
In winter, I see the snowman arrive,
As my mom makes hot cocoa inside.
For this I have many reasons,
I guess I love all the seasons.

Kylee Rosenbaum
Age: 10

MY GOAT CLOVER

My goat Clover is very good.
She likes to chew on lots of wood.
She likes to jump around and around
on the hill and on the ground.
She likes to eat leaves off trees,
She likes to eat leaves in the breeze.
I took her to the county fair
and there were lots of people there.
Judges thought she did very well,
all of her ribbons I can show and tell.
Clover is my best friend
and we will be together 'til the very end.

Kellie Boo
Age: 9

MY CAPTOR

Surveying the landscape
I see only death
And evil before me
With blood on his breath
His claws seeking carnage
His fangs seeking pain
Crushing all who oppose it
His terror will reign
Consumed with fear
Yet unable to run
He lashes out for me
His bidding be done
Unable to escape
The ending is near
My blood rushes from me
My fate now seems clear
I have bowed to this evil
I have failed to try
My weakness destroys me
As I lie here to die

Michael Rinkovsky

SCHOOL OR PLAY

Paper, pencils, erasers, markers!
School, school, school!
It's everywhere! but then, I think,
what would we do without school?
We'd play all day in sun or rain,
have fun with friends, say some puns.
But how would we learn, always out, never in?
There would be no paper, pencils, erasers, markers.
But we'd never get anywhere,
never smarter, then I wonder,
What would we do without school?

Alyssa Thordarson
Age: 9

WHO ARE MY FRIENDS

I wish I knew who my friends were.
I only try to get along with everyone.
I only try to fit in with everyone.
I wish I knew who to call my friends

When I keep quiet
They say I think I am better than them
They say that I don't want to get along
They say I don't want to get to know them

When I joke around with them.
They say I am causing trouble.
They will take things out of content.
They will say things to make me look bad.

I don't say things about other people.
I always try to find the good in them.
I just want to get along with everyone.

I only want to be treated the way I treat you
If I treat you with respect.
If I treat you as a person with feelings.
If I treat you as a person that can get hurt
with words or actions
Then I hope you'll call me your friend.

Sean Patrick Mahoney
Age: 14

GOLDEN STATE

Travel, fly, travel, fly

The Airport
Loud not so friendly crowds,
Loud noises, frantic people,
Escalators that run underground,
And has a lot of neon lights.

Travel, drive, travel, drive

San Francisco
Plenty of good restaurants
The Golden Gate Bridge,
Fisherman's Wharf,
Plenty of salt water taffy.

Travel, drive, travel, drive

The Motel
Two wonderfully warm pools,
Lots of fog, lots of swimming,
Plenty of polite clerks.

Travel, drive, travel, drive

The Cousin's House
Lots of friends, cool streams to wade
Lots of bike riding, and exploring,
A big boulder that you could climb.

Travel, drive, travel, drive
Napa Valley Winery
Happy crowds, bright, sunny day,
Red and white wine, luscious green,
Grape vines, cool moist cellars,
Big and small wooden kegs of old wine.

Travel, drive, travel, drive

The Ocean
Plenty of cool, freezing water,
Lots of sand, jellyfish, and shells,
A few moist and musty caves,
A few crabs and a lot of sea gulls.

Travel, hike, travel, hike

The Cliff
Plenty of rocks and seals,
Lots of sea gulls and a strong breeze,
And a few dolphins.

Travel, hike, travel, hike

The Lighthouse
Hundreds of stairs,
Steep cliffs, big boats,
Glorious views.

Travel, drive, travel, drive

The Redwoods
Red-barked giants that reach to the stars,
long, narrow, twisting, curving roads

that reach to the sky,
Long exhausting hikes, and cool streams.

Travel, drive, travel, drive

The Big Dipper
Mouth-watering ice cream,
Flavors so good it feels like heaven,
A gumball machine that if you get a white one
You win five certificate bucks. (I won!)

Travel, drive, travel, drive

China Town
A really good restaurant called
Oriental Pearl, a big busy park,
Large but happy crowds,
Great treasures

Travel, fly, travel, fly

Rob Coffey
Age: 12

As I walked
along the riverbank
I heard an old gray crow.

Its beak was chipped.
Its eyes were sad.
Its feathers browned with age.

As it looked up at me
it seemed to want to come.
Yet as I walked closer
it seemed to shy away.

The bird flew off cawing,
like I had done it wrong.

I watched the bird fly away
and disappear into the sun.

That was the last time
I saw the old gray crow.

Kelly G. Kilgore
Age: 11

THE LONE WOLF

The lone wolf sits howling in the snow,
listening for signs of his pack,
for he has nowhere to go.

The lone wolf sits howling in the snow,
there is nothing but silence,
and the wind begins to blow.

The lone wolf sits howling in the snow,
he hears a noise, turns his back,
and sees eyes that glow.

He doesn't run, he's not afraid,
for, once again, he's returned
to his mighty wolf pack.

Kimberly R. Miller
Age: 11

DOGS

Dogs are better than frogs,
And better than cows,
And better than hogs,
Dogs.

Jazmin Cardenas
Age: 11

SCHOOL

School is cool,
School is like a golden rule.
High school is a ridicule,
School is cool
So boogie on down to school.

Jennifer Wintek
Age: 10

THE FLOWERS IN THE GRAVEYARD

He's got beautiful blue irises
and golden petals around his face
On the inside his pain rises
he then wilts and slows his pace

The flower in the graveyard
he's so handsome in a life so hard
I'll comfort him and put him in the light
I'll water him and watch him through the night

Fall is coming and the cold wind will blow
and my beautiful flower will no longer grow
he is becoming weak and his color is starting to fade
then soon his roots will fill the gap
in the empty hole I've made

It is coming to an end
and I'm losing my only friend
he shall now take his place by the baby's breath
He'll be my loving flower in the graveyard in death.

Emily Armstrong
Age: 14

My name is Lance.
I don't love to dance.
People say that I have ants in my pants.
I love to drink pop.
I'll never stop.
I love cake.
But hate to rake.

Lance Taylor

G lowing
L ight
O f
S hiny
S un
Y ahoo!

Nicole Marie Taylor

DOLPHINS

Dolphins in the water,
swim dolphins swim.
They go down where the fish swim,
where you can go and win a swim with them.
A ring of dolphins swim all around
dolphins swim up and down all around the water.
Dolphins jump into the air high,
into the air where the birds fly high in the air.

Chrystal Bealor
Age: 14

CATS AND BATS

I love cats,
I hate bats.
Cats are cool,
Bats drool.

Cats are nice,
They chase mice.
Bats eat cats,
And eat rats.

I love cats,
I hate bats.
'Cause cats are better,
Than bats!

Sarah Elizabeth Greene
Age: 11

SOMEWHERE IN MY MEMORY

Somewhere in my memory
There's a little boy called Jeremy
He lives all alone in the sodded house
And he doesn't even talk to the little mouse

The little mouse has dapple fur
And he doesn't like to hear a cat purr
He lives all alone in the sodded house
And he doesn't even talk to the little louse

The little louse lives on a pole
He never even sees another living soul
He lives all alone in the sodded house
In the sodded house alone

Megan Elizabeth Cosman
Age: 10

ZERO

With a zero batting average,
She has trouble, it is true.
But when she hit a homer,
The stands yelled yahoo!

Casey Webb
Age: 10

I love waffles,
I eat them stack after stack,
Pack after pack.
With syrup and butter
Then they taste better.
My mom keeps making 'em and making 'em,
I keep eating 'em and eating 'em.

Victoria Budak

FALL

When the wind blows it shakes the trees
The sun rises at the crack of dawn
The geese fly south for the winter
Trees turn colors of red, gold, and brown
I have been there before, and I never forgot
What a wonderful and pretty sight

Leaves fall from the trees
So my dad makes a pile, for my sister and I
After school we have races,
Of who can jump the farthest
I have been there before and I never forgot
What a wild and fun thing it was

My neighbors close their pool, for it is too cold
They will miss swimming, for their pool is closed
It now turns cold, for no more swimming
We will miss the summer, for fall is coming!

Jacquelyn A. Stillman
Age: 10

VETERANS DAY

Thank you Mister,
Thank you Miss,
You give me joy,
You give me bliss,
You served America,
Proud and strong
Through pain
And strain,
You did not complain.
You went to Vietnam;
You went to Germany.
To those that have died,
I give you my sympathy.
Many were injured,
Many were missed.
To all those
You are truly blessed.
Thank you Mister,
Thank you Miss,
To all the deceased
We truly miss.

Christian Ameling
Age: 13

THE EARTH

The surface brown and showy,
sometimes flat and snowy.

This great earth of ours,
sure is better than planet Mars.

Some people say earth is small,
but I know better, more than all.

Earth is such a great place,
where you can live in your own space.

I pick planet Earth above all!

Kevin Pazour
Age: 13

LUNCH

I like lunch.
I just can't wait
to have a munch.

I like lunch.
Some of my food
just goes crunch!

I like lunch.
I put my wrappers
in a bunch.

Adrian Rose
Age: 10

Dad
nice funny
laughing smiling playing
love riding bikes together
Man

Rachel Elizabeth Anderson

ART SUPPLIES

Once my art supplies came to life
I could not believe my eyes
They said to me
"We have fun just watch and see."
How could that be?
My pencil said
"Why can't I be red?"
I'm only an ugly yellow,
So I won't get a fellow.
How sad!

Jill Krieger
Age: 9

NATALIE

I have a sister,
Natalie is her name.
She really likes to play a lot of games.

From tag to tennis,
dance to hide-and-go-seek,
although she is a menace.

My sister can be very kind
then again, maybe not.
She always has to make me find,
her in a hiding spot!

That is all I want to say,
I'll tell you more another day.
Because we're going out to play.

Christina Csonka
Age: 10

THE GREEN MONSTER

I woke up one day,
I can't tell if it's Monday,
I had to go to school one way,
I saw a green monster,
It was so mean,
You probably know it wasn't slim,
He had red eyes,
And an evil grin.
You probably know if you saw him.
He asked, "Would someone
Go to the dance with me?"
I said, "No, I don't. I'd never go with you!"
He cried, he pleaded.
I said, "No, even if I said hello."
He said, "I'm going home!"
He crushed the school.
He crushed my home,
He crushed everything,
Oh, no!
He went home,
I was sad, I think I'll never be glad.

Sabrina Lee Atchley
Age: 10

CAT

I am a cat not a bat.
Nor a hat or a rat.
I am a cat.
Do not sit on me.
I have claws and a tail to whack.
If you smack you will get a whack.
I can whack you in your back.
I love my cat.
I love my cat because he does not whack.
I love my cat!
She is not a bat.
My cat.

Reane Alegre
Age: 10

I WISH I HAD A DOG

I wish I had a dog pink and purple
  and with a little tail too.
I wish I had a dog that would kiss me too.
I wish I had a little dog too.
He would be so very nice to you.
He would like to be with you.

Megan Fortner
Age: 8

MY WISH

If I could make a wish,
I'd like to be a fish.
I would flip and splash,
And probably move in a flash.
I would swim 'round and 'round,
Without making a sound.
Of course I would be wiggling,
And perhaps even swiggling.
I would be swimming in the clear,
That nobody could hear.

Brian McGuire
Age: 11

MY BELOVED TEXACO

I am in love
With the Texaco station
And bore people with
My long conversations
About my beloved
Texaco station.

Unlike the rest
It is very clean
But it does still reek
With brown gasoline
Yet the people who work there
Are not very mean.

So I love Texaco
It's better than the rest
And also in Texaco
There isn't much mess
Because overall
It's best in the west.

Joseph Livarchik
Age: 14

MY MOTHER

My mom is special and loves me
she has to wear glasses to see
she does not like to cook
but she has lots of books.

My mom is very smart
when we go shopping she fills up the cart
she is vey nice
but she doesn't like mice.

Jaimie Huguenard
Age: 9

MY SUNSHINE

Hills are green as grass
Roses are red as apples,
But you are my sunshine
Forever and always.

Through the days and the nights
Dreaming of your sights,
I realize the truth
That I love you now and always.

Laura Malnar
Age: 14

If I were a bird
I'd fly everywhere
from the mountains to the hillsides.

The moment I had reached
my destination,
I'd just keep going.

I could see what I want,
go anywhere I want,
and be happy all the time.

I'd sleep when I am tired
eat when I am hungry,
and go anywhere at anytime.

Rachel Thomas
Age: 13

ROCKETS

I dream of rockets soaring in the sky,
I also wonder, "Why can't I?"
I wish I could be the commander of a flight,
But I know that cannot happen overnight.

Timothy Jarzombek
Age: 11

A STAR FROM AFAR

There once was a star,
it came from afar,
it was born from a nebular,
and that star,
that came from afar,
was the brightest star,
that came from afar,
that star was my friend.

Alexander Jay Popovich
Age: 11

Autumn autumn
Swaying, falling, changing trees.
Scaring, frightening, screaming Halloween.
Falling, racking, burning leaves.
Autumn autumn

Kristin Knowlton
Age: 11

MOM

My mom is cool
She loves to bake
She likes to take me places
My mom is cool
She likes to talk
She loves me very much
My mom is cool
She always has time for me
My mom is very cool.

Carrie Highlan
Age: 11

I wonder where life
is going to take me.
I wonder where death
is going to take me.
I wonder where Spike
is going to take me.

Madeline Weiler

VALENTINE

Last year my dog died
I was going to break down and cry
My sister was bawling
And I was ruined.

Nobody even cares
So how many people care
Just me and my family
Sitting in the air.

Courtney Saurborn
Age: 10

BATS

B lack
A ll fly in the sky
T he bats sleep in the day
S cary bats

Venci Popov

MY BUS

My bus is very stinky,
it's also very clinky.

If you rode my bus
you just might bust.

If you rode my bus you'd know,
that we go very slow.

The bus ride is loud
since there's a big crowd.

During the ride
this kid started to cry.

This is my bus,
don't worry it won't rust.

Tyler Doane

Teamwork
shoulder pads
jerseys cleats helmets
offense defensive goal touchdown
Crowd

Jeremy Rutherford
Age: 10

CHRISTMAS

Christmas
Colored lights on trees
Cookies baking
Christmas caroling
Turkey
Presents
Christmas

Eric Swiatkowski
Age: 7

Wintry
white flakes
steaming hot cocoa
burning fireplace comforters hats
Sashes

Jennifer Tucker
Age: 10

A TRIBUTE TO HORSES

Being a horse rider
Is my one and only dream
Every girl must feel that way,
So unrealistic it may seem.
I think about being a horse rider
Every single day.
I'm trying to achieve my biggest goal
In every possible way.
I want to fly on Pegasus
All the way through the stars
I want to fly to Pluto
Then land on top of Mars.
I want to fly over sparkling oceans
Flying like the wind,
Then I want to get back on the horse
And do it all over again.
If there is anything
That I would like more than a Porsche
It's my very own pony or horse.

Stephanie Healy
Age: 11

POEM FOR MY GIRL

You may not be able to cure a wound or a broken bone,
but I know for sure you will always be my girl.
I say this to you now so you will remember me,
for when you and I die we can have unity,
but right now for the moment let's have our best days
in every way shape or form and live them day by day.
I love you with all my heart and to you I write this rhyme
so you'll remember me 'til the end of time.

Matthew J. Schroeder
Age: 14

School
spelling teacher
books pencils gym
recess lunch music art
Learning

Brandon Potter
Age: 10

THUNDERHEAD!

Thunderhead thunderhead
you're so gray,
please don't storm today.
Mama's got the clothes hanging outside,
we all want them to get dry.
Thunderhead thunderhead please go away,
you can come another day.

Alexis R. Rensink
Age: 10

Freddy the frog
sat on a log
one by one in the hot hot sun
he ate the flies as they flew by

Richard E. Burch Sherrick
Age: 8

THE MAN ON THE MOON

Once there was a man named Scott Dune.
He flew to the moon.
He found it so hot he turned to a prune.
Many men flew to the moon
and found it so hot they turned into a prune.
They make up the man on the moon.

Claudia Lyster
Age: 10

WINTER DAYS

Snow is falling down.
Snowmen dancing all around.
Sledding down the hills.

Erica Leimer
Age: 10

CHEERLEADER STACEY

There once was a cheerleader named Stacey Cheer.
She cheered and did cartwheels.
To get her energy she drank root beer,
Her birthday was on New Year's.
She did cartwheels three in a row
And amazed all the girls in the world.
Finally this -- the story of Stacey Cheer.

Monserrat Miramontes

Birthday
November's earliest
Wake up stimulated
We begin to commend
Gifts

Seun Emmanuel Ojelade
Age: 10

LOOK UP

Look up and see the sky.
Look up and see the sun.
Look up and see the moon.
Look up and see the stars.
Look up and see the clouds.
Look up and see a creation.

Kathleen Van't Hof
Age: 12

SNOW

The snow is falling
So pretty and elegant,
A sign of Christmas.

Caryn Sknerski
Age: 10

BASEBALL

Baseball is fun to play.
To throw and catch.
And to hit the ball away.
The pitcher throws a strike.
And the batter faints.
The batter runs to base the umpire says you're out.

William Ortiz
Age: 10

DOGS

I have a dog named Mazy
Some days she's kind of lazy
Other days she runs and plays
I think I like her better that way.

Julie Furman
Age: 10

PUPPY

Puppy, puppy by my side,
Uses the bathroom outside.
Plays with me in my house,
Paws at my face and mouth.
You'll be my best friend forever and ever.

Anna Nichole Crownover

Snowflakes
white, glittering
soothing, freezing, sparkling
snowflakes turn into freezing ice
Snow

Morgan Kudrecki
Age: 10

MOM

When my mom and I play
She always makes my day.
When my mom reads
She always thinks of good deeds.
When my mom makes me lunch
She always gives me punch.

Ryan A. Kettle
Age: 7

Nintendo
super games
playing, using, buying
you can play it at home
Awesome!

Ryan Rich
Age: 9

PUMPKINS

P umpkin pies are good to eat
U nder pumpkin lids we put candles
M y mom makes pumpkin pies
P umpkins can have scary faces
K ids make jack-o'-lanterns
I like pumpkin seeds
N ew costumes for Halloween

Ellybeth J. Castañeda
Age: 6

COLORS

The world is many colors
Blue, green, yellow, orange, and brown
That makes the world pretty

Celena M. Matalin
Age: 10

LEAVES

L eaves are fun
E verybody rakes
A utumn is fun
V ery colorful
E verybody plays in the leaves
S o let's go play in the leaves

Shaylah Shepard
Age: 6

FOOTBALL

Football football it is cool.
You get to catch a football too.
You get to make touchdowns too.
You also get to make touchdowns for the team.
The coolest thing is that you get
to win the championship.

Joshua Swindle
Age: 9

AUTUMN

A pples are good
U nder the leaves kids play
T rick-or-treat
U p in the sky birds fly south
M oms make good pumpkin pies
N ew costumes for Halloween

Katie Christine Lawson
Age: 6

LUCKY

My dog's name is Lucky
and lucky he is.
He jumps on my bed
and he loves to lick me.

Jake Kryda
Age: 8

THE BIG RACE

The crowd is roaring,
Rain is pouring,
And I am getting ready to race.
When I got to my starting position,
I decided that, I didn't want to be in the competition.
Then I remembered that I like to race,
So when the starting gun went off,
I had a smile on my face.

Matt Stahura
Age: 11

PANCAKES

They taste good
With syrup
When you eat them
Your tummy is full.

Dustin McCoy
Age: 9

IT'S RAINING

"It's raining like dogs and cats"
That's what my mother always says.
But I wonder if she always says that when it rains.
So I close my eyes and say "Stop!"
But I have no luck.
So I get in the van and say "I wish I had good luck."

Elena Cuellar
Age: 8

APPLES

Apples are red
Apples are blue
One for me
And one for you!

Katherine Banasiak
Age: 9

WHERE DID YOU GO?

It is time for dinner, but where is Lulu?
Oh where can she be. Oh! Lulu!
Where are you?
Come out Lulu!
She's not in the bathroom!
Oh!!!
Lulu, where are you?
Out came Lulu.
Gosh, can't a girl get some rest?

Emily Long
Age: 8

Leaves of all colors
Brown, red, gold, orange and purple
Are falling way down.

Matt Louden

BOTANICALS

Green,
Brown,
Growing in ground,
Water with care;
They'll bring blooms to share.
Straight and tall,
Heeding nature's call
To reach for the sun.

Joshua Carlascio
Age: 13

There was an old man.
He played with the hose.
He died because he squirted water up his nose.

Jeremy Godek

ALONE

Alone
majestic
towering the earth
reaching for the sky
like a plant reaching for light
taunting man to reach its heights
cold, barren, bringing man so close to
the Creator of both the man and nature
so alone, so majestic; this they call Everest.

Nathan Gardner
Age: 13

Poems
hard, short
writing, rhyming, tiring
have to think it
Shakespeare

Paul Grubbs

THANKSGIVING IS...

Thanksgiving is turkey covered with glaze.
A time of joy.
A time of thanks.
Pulling a wishbone.
A family time.
A time of beautifully covered leaves.

Benjamin U. Van Sickle

Soccer
worldwide fun game
dribbling kicking passing
compete motivated happy
A Sport

Larry Tylenda

FEELINGS

A feeling deep inside of me
Is something that no one can see.
The smile you see
Is not really me
And that laugh that you hear
Is just a mere tear
That drops from my face
Nobody can trace.

Kristen Rubin
Age: 11

REEL THEM IN

Cast, cast catch those
Bluegill and large mouth bass
Catch those muskie fight them in
Take a picture and realize them back
Bring your lures don't forget
Bring your poles
Fish by yourself fish with a friend
Go down to the lake and reel them in!

Jessica Govert
Age: 11

THE DEMON

The Demon has been here,
The Demon will come there,
She will destroy me,
By tearing me to pieces,
I just shouldn't have gotten involved.
She has been here once before,
And when she left I said,
"Quote the Raven, 'Nevermore'."
Now she's gotten me again,
Caught by her immoral, immortal strength,
This time with depression as her weapon,
She tortures me as if on the torture rack.

They always try to snipe me,
Yeah, and get me while I'm down,
She's struck below the belt this time,
This time she went too far,
Helped by my own good friend.

Now she lurks in my closet,
Or hides in my drawer,
And she waits, waits until I'm down,
And now she's ready for gore,
She's moving in for the kill.
But I repel her, somehow.

She sends me into war with myself,
Until,
I find another, and when that time comes,
I can guarantee you; I'll quote that Raven,
"Nevermore."

The Demon is the aftershock,
The Demon is the war,
The Demon is my bloody rage,
The Demon is my depression, my destruction,
That is until, I destroy her.
The Demon can also be the woman I love,
The Demon can be anyone, just because,
The Front Line Is Everywhere.
And with this I part and,
Once again I quote the Raven,
"Nevermore."

Ben Stover
Age: 13

PEAK-A-BOO BEE

Peak-a-boo I see you, but you
don't see me, why because I am a
bee you see. Don't be mad and don't
be sad. It doesn't matter if you
win or lose, you're good at peak-a-boo,
just not as good as me. Why? Because
I am a bee you can't see. "OK," but
guess what, I see you bee that I
can't see. You're sitting on my knee.

Nicholas Thompson
Age: 11

PARENTS

P is for patience which they have a lot of.
A is for adoring me as a little girl.
R is for helping me relax when I'm sick.
E is for ending arguments between me and my sister.
N is for helping me when I need help.
T is for telling me answers to my questions.
S is for sending love to me.

Elizabeth Bombagetti
Age: 10

THE SKY IS THE LIMIT

The wind is blowing over the trees
The bees are buzzing oh those bees
Don't worry they won't hurt you
They're very friendly you see
God made all creatures just for you and me
I love to sing about when God made things right
There is no limit you can soar to any height
When you're feeling sad and blue
God will come and help you through

Lorna Slupczynski
Age: 10

MY CAT

My cat is small,
she is funny,
she's not tall,
and she talks.

She's not a normal cat.

Marija Nikolai

MAYBE SOMEDAY

Maybe someday I'll dance with you
Maybe not now
Maybe not later
But maybe someday will do the mashed potato
But maybe that day you will not like
To do the mashed potato
But maybe you would like to do the jitterbug
Maybe not on stage
Maybe not in a ballroom
But we will do it in a theater.

Brittany Ann Bonaguro
Age: 11

APPLES

Apples are sweet.
Apples can be sour.
Apples are a sour and sweet treat.
Apples sometimes can be tricky
because they're so sticky.

Audra Langbehn
Age: 9

AUTUMN

Autumn is great.
It is never late.
Autumn is fun.
Sometimes there is a sun.
The leaves are different colors.
Like red, orange, and brown,
But they always fall down.

Hillary Bade
Age: 10

HOCKEY

H ockey is a fun sport.
O ver and over you play without tiring.
C ool ice is hard when you hit the floor.
K nocked into the wall, get back up.
E nough of this you say and you knock the person
  into the wall.
Y es, do it again and again and again.

Matt Davis
Age: 9

THE BEACH

I lie by the bay.
I look at the pretty sea.
It is amazing.

Scott Noth
Age: 9

FRIENDS

F riends are fun.
R espect them and they will respect you.
I have a lot of friends do you?
E vents can happen with friends.
N iceness helps to be a bigger friend.
D reams you can share.
S ecrets you should save to be a friend.

Elizabeth Anne Langston
Age: 8

CHRISTMAS

Christmas
Stockings, angels, and Christmas trees
Cinnamon
Carolers
Cookies and candy canes
Presents
Christmas

Erica Gorton
Age: 7

IF I HAD A PUPPY

If I had a puppy he would be playful and jumpy,
He would run and play all day,
If I had a puppy,
When I would get home from school
He would greet me very sweetly,
He would give me lots and lots of kisses,
Don't you think he would be a sweety?

Devin Holme
Age: 9

HALLOWEEN

Halloween
Trick-or-treaters everywhere
Leaves burning in the air
Children screaming here and there
Candy and treats are for me
Doorbells ringing, ding, ding, ding
Halloween is so neat!

Kimberlee Koehler
Age: 8

CANDY

Candy is yummy!
You know who told me? my tummy.
My favorite is a gummy.
It doesn't matter if it's rainy or sunny,
Candy makes me act funny,
I even feed it to my pet bunny.
Do you have any extra money?
'Cause I'm all out of gummies!

Nicoletta Aliferakis
Age: 9

WINTER

Cold one morning, I awoke at dawn,
And where had all the grass gone?
Covered with sheets of white snow,
The grass will no longer grow.
Sledding down the icy hills,
Children shout from the thrills.
Christmas carols have people humming,
And before you know it, Good Ol' St. Nick is coming!

Gretchen Luegers
Age: 13

MY GOLDFISH

I have two goldfish,
I keep them in a tank not a dish.
A fish has a backbone.
I have two fish, so they are never alone.
They are about ten months old.
Ronnie is shy, Goldie is bold.

David Lambka
Age: 8

SUNSET INTO THE WATER

Sunset, sunset in the sky,
God please bless the sunset as the days go by,
God bless the water so cold and deep,
That the sun goes into the water as I sleep.

Jhana Rolfe
Age: 10

TITANIC

The ship of dreams Titanic used to be,
A great ship that roamed the sea.
Too big a ship, too small a rudder,
That is how the big ship shuddered.
All the people run with fears,
Many passengers lost their dears.

Lynne M. Stanko
Age: 8

THE CAT THAT WANTS MY LUNCH!

Everyday my cat bites my nose.
When I wake up she runs down to the kitchen.
I went to get some lunch she ran to get my sandwich.
I pushed her away so she wouldn't get my sandwich.
The next day she will be in a cage.
So, now I can eat my lunch in peace.

Craig Swetkey
Age: 10

MY CAT TIBBINS

We have a cat we call her Mama's
She once lived in the Bahamas
And now she chases llamas
She'll do anything for dramas
With those four out of one scratching claws
And those sixteen out of two sharp fat teeth
Stuck in her jaws.

Sarah McComb
Age: 9

C hocolate chip cookies baking for me
H anging ornaments from our tree
R udolph shines his nose so bright
I dream about Santa Claus tonight
S leigh bells ringing in the snow
T oday's the day we are all aglow
M aking a list for Santa to read
A sking him for all kinds of toys I need
S haring all of our love and joy.

Haylee Lynn Ksiazek

SPORTS

I like to play many sports
Especially on basketball courts.
I hit a baseball with a bat,
While I wear my black Nike hat.
I like to throw a ball,
While shopping in the mall.
Some people think sports are fun,
Too bad this poem is done.

John P. Kiger
Age: 9

ALL ABOUT MY PET GUINEA PIG, REGGIE!

My guinea pig likes to eat.
And it likes to chomp to the beat!
My guinea pig is really called a "Cavey."
I think it likes biscuits and gravy!

Kevin S. Scott
Age: 6

BASKETBALL STUFF

Basketball is fun
Everyone gets to run
Brick, miss, make
It is just for fun
If you win or if you lose
Basketball is fun for everyone

Michael Westgate
Age: 8

B randon is my name.
R esponsible is what I am.
A 's are the grade.
N eatness is a must.
D ogs are my favorite pet.
O ranges are what I like.
N iceness is the best.

Brandon Lee Lintner
Age: 6

FALL

When the cold comes,
BEHOLD!
Here comes the cold.
All people are nice.
When houses smell like spice.
When it's cold.

Julia Spann
Age: 10

NICKY

I like my dog Nicky.
When he eats he is so picky.
When he is happy he wags his tail.
When he is sad he starts to wail.
His fur is all black.
He is so small he can fit in a sack.

Denise Naparla
Age: 7

In 1492, Columbus sailed the ocean blue.
A storm came,
And he hit a wave,
That was bigger than a cave.
He tried very hard to see if there was gold,
But he found out it was really cold.
He found land,
And he was really grand
That he could touch sand.
That's the end of my story,
But not the end of Columbus' glory.

Brittany Richardson
Age: 10

MY DOG

I like my dog.
She likes to sleep.
She is strong.
Sometimes she's mean. Sometimes she's nice.
She hates balls. She likes cars.
She loves food and walks.
She is also fast.
I like my dog.

Donald R. Brown
Age: 10

CHRISTOPHER COLUMBUS

In 1492, Columbus sailed the ocean blue.
The pirates came,
And he put them to shame.
Then a storm approached,
But they didn't get soaked.
He found a perfect beach,
When the sun looked like a peach.
If you don't think it's true,
You're wrong 'cause I do!

Jamie Lynne Detmar
Age: 10

Autumn
fall shades
tan maroon gold
chilly crunchy crisp cool
Nature

Jonathan Seles
Age: 10

CHRISTMAS EVE

It bites my skin like a
ripping wind. It is the
day before Christmas Eve.
I hear sleigh bells ringing
and families singing
against the glorious
winter
night.

Stephanie Rettig
Age: 11

October
chilly windy
leaves change shades
pumpkins Halloween party costumes
Frightening

Eugene Bohannon
Age: 10

BUSY SPIDER

Spiders are so neat
Arachnids do a lot of work
Making the web
To catch bugs
They must lurk
In the light of the moon.

Mara Ofengender
Age: 8

WHERE'S MY HAT?!

There was a man who was fat
He always wore a hat
It was a fact -- he had no hair
Without a hat, his head felt bare
He was looking for his favorite one
He saw it in the corner, looking kind of flat
When he looked inside he saw his cat
Oh no! How could he put that on his head
When his cat made it into a bed?!

Adam Huizenga
Age: 11

SPIDER

S pinning on my web
P rey, come all day
I catch them in my web
D ie, die, my insect dinner
E nemies beware of my trap
R un far away!

Haley Sorenson
Age: 8

R eally cool
A wesome
I nteresting
N ice
B right
O dd
W ow

Bridget Marczewski

Sun
light, bright
shining, burning, scorching
fiery, hot, rocky, cool
Armstrong, discovery, orbiting
dark, shadowy
Moon

Amy Gyure

MY IMAGINATION

A kitten and a puppy
in the garden,
reading to some purple flowers
and a beautiful orange butterfly,
whispering
like magic
in my imagination.

Lauren Comer
Age: 10

SHIPS AND CRACKERS

Ships and crackers are not a good mixture.
Ships sail across the sea, but crackers don't.
Crackers are eaten, but ships aren't.
So to get a good mixture,
you can carve the cracker into a ship
and then you can eat it like you really ate a ship.
I don't know about ships though.
So that means I really just don't know.

Allison Nicole Kowalkowski
Age: 8

T ugboat
I ceberg
T all
A wesome
N ice
I ron
C old

Kurt Schuzer

J olly
E xcited
N ice
I ce cream lover
S illy
E xtraordinary

Jenise Flores

WEATHER

Weather, weather.
What's the weather?
Who knows what the weather is like?
Can you guess the weather?
I bet you can.
Look at the Weather Channel.

Aaron Brown
Age: 8